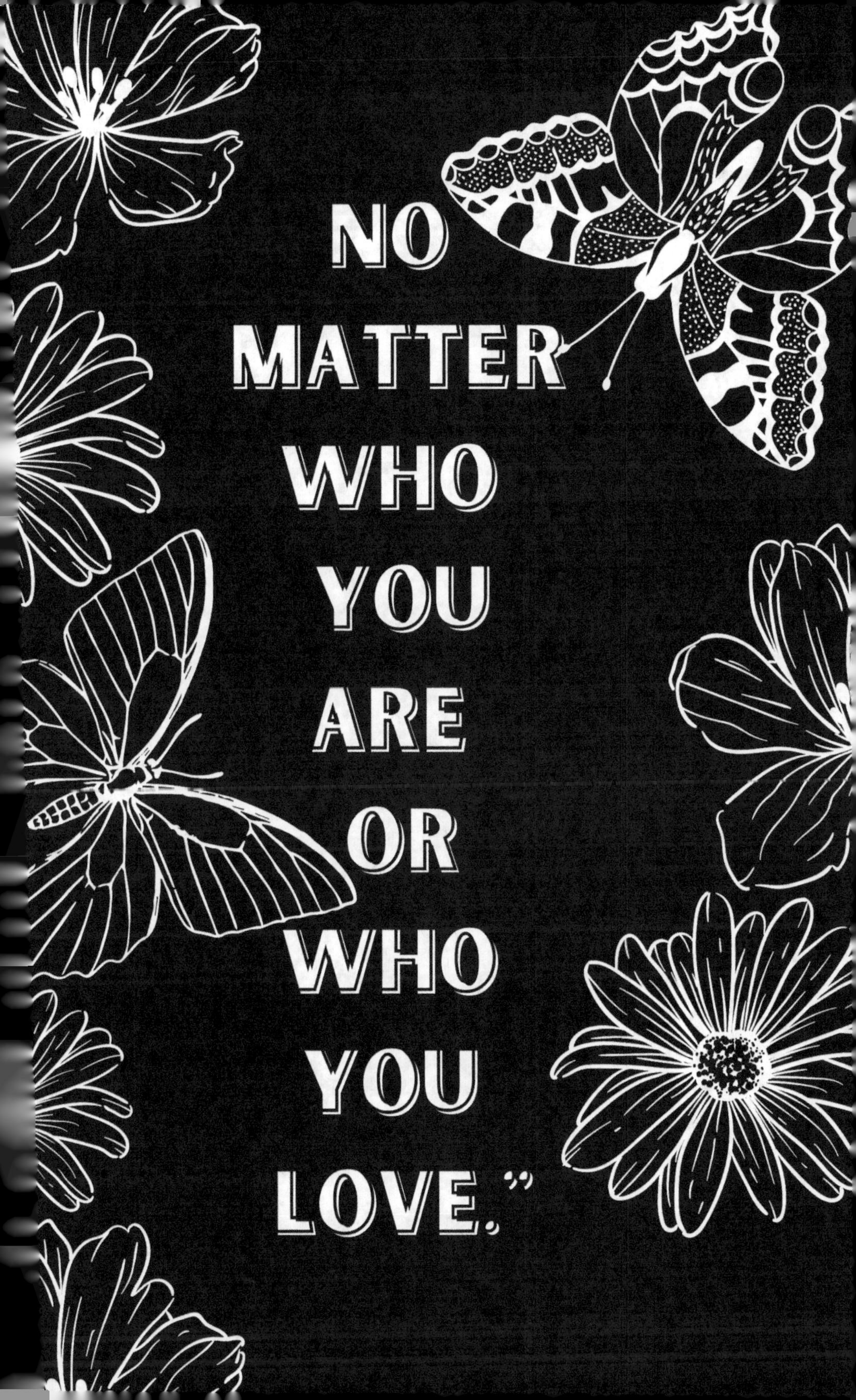
NO
MATTER
WHO
YOU
ARE
OR
WHO
YOU
LOVE."

"LOVE HAS NO BOUNDARIES, NO LIMITS, AND NO DISCRIMINATION."

"Love is a human right, not a privilege.

Embrace it, celebrate it, and never apologize for it."

BEING TRUE TO
YOURSELF AND
THOSE
you love is
the
greatest
act
OF COURAGE AND
STRENGTH."

Be proud of who you are and who you love.
Don't let anyone else dictate your happiness

Love is a journey, not a destination.
It's a choice that you make every day to be kind, understanding, and accepting."

"Love is the foundation of a strong, healthy, and happy relationship."

"Love is the most powerful force in the universe.

IT CAN CONQUER ALL FEAR, HATRED, AND BIGOTRY."

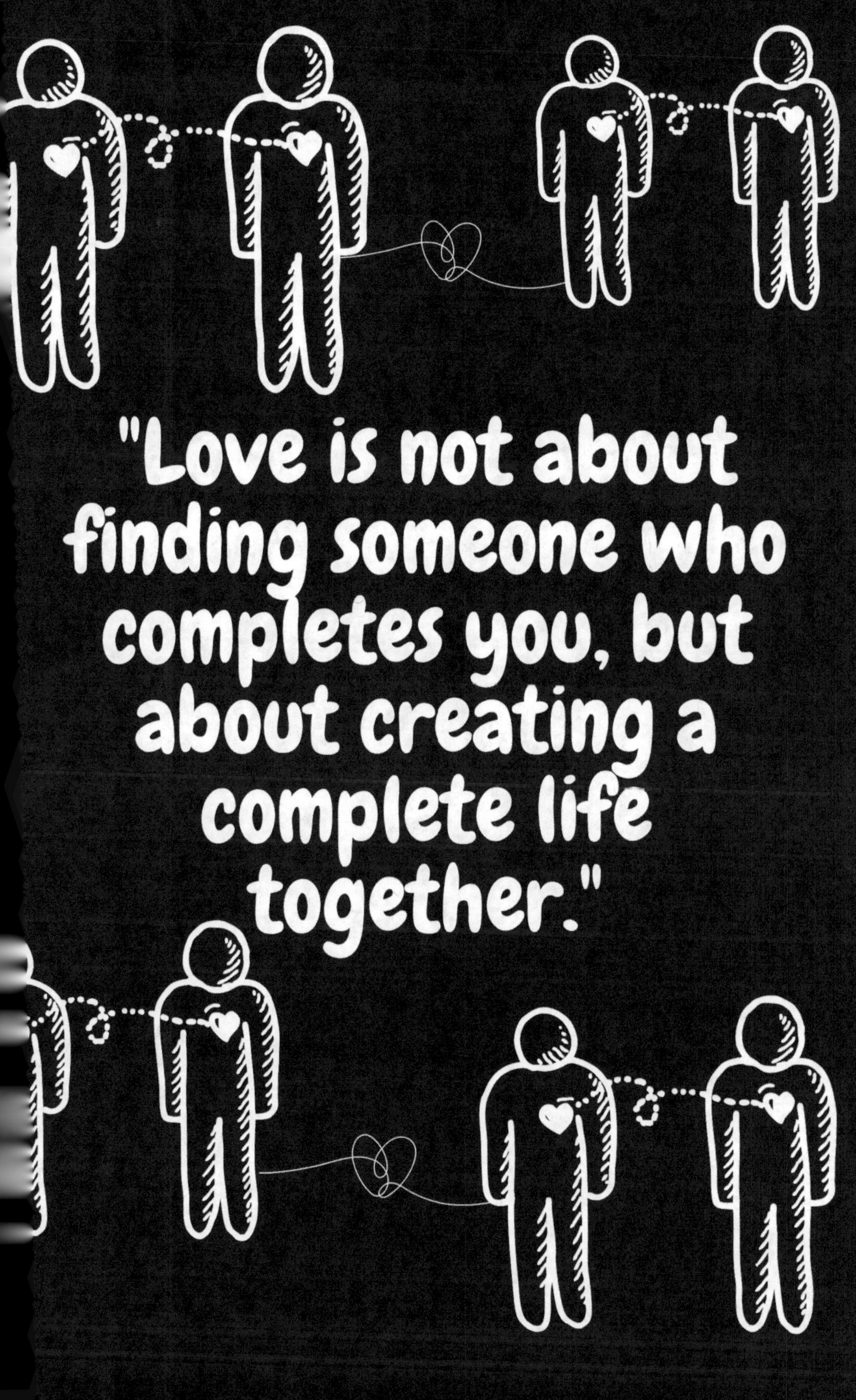
"Love is not about finding someone who completes you, but about creating a complete life together."

"Love is about acceptance, not perfection. It's about embracing each other's flaws and differences"

. "LOVE IS A BEAUTIFUL, POWERFUL THING.

IT SHOULD BE CELEBRATED, NOT FEARED OR DISCRIMINATED AGAINST."

"YOU ARE NOT ALONE. THERE ARE PEOPLE OUT THERE WHO LOVE AND ACCEPT YOU FOR WHO YOU ARE."

"LOVE IS THE GLUE THAT BINDS US TOGETHER, THROUGH THE GOOD TIMES AND THE BAD."
GLUE

"Love is a
beautiful thing
that should be
celebrated and
shared with the
world."

"LOVE KNOWS NO GENDER OR SEXUAL ORIENTATION.

It is a universal force that connects us all."

YOU ARE NOT DEFINED BY YOUR GENDER OR SEXUAL ORIENTATION.
YOU ARE DEFINED BY YOUR HEART AND YOUR SOUL."

"LOVE
IS
A
CHOICE"

"You can't control who you love,
BUT YOU CAN CONTROL HOW YOU LOVE."

"Being true to yourself is the most courageous thing you can do."

"LOVE IS A FORCE THAT CAN CHANGE THE WORLD.
IT CAN BRING PEOPLE TOGETHER AND INSPIRE POSITIVE CHANGE."

Thank You